Samsung Galaxy S4

A Complete Step by Step Guide

Disclaimer

No part of this eBook can be transmitted or reproduced in any form including print, electronic, photocopying, scanning, mechanical or recording without prior written permission from the author.

All information, ideas and guidelines presented here are for educational purposes only.

While the author has taken utmost efforts to ensure the accuracy of the written content, all readers are advised to follow information mentioned herein at their own risk. The author cannot be held responsible for any personal or commercial damage caused by misinterpretation of information. All readers are encouraged to seek professional advice when needed.

Unveiling Samsung Galaxy S4

Samsung or its 'Galaxy S' series do not need any introduction. If you have been a Samsung fan, you must have an idea about the spectacular range of phones that are available under this banner. Adding to the 'Galaxy S' family this year is their latest Samsung Galaxy S4.

This book will cover all the details about this phone that can be used as a user manual. Most of the features mentioned here are exclusive for Galaxy S4. In fact, you will also find step by step tutorials for some complicated setups to help you get started with your new, exciting Galaxy S4.

Keep reading until you completely fall in love with your phone!

Other Titles By This Author Include…

http://www.amazon.com/dp/B00ALC9OHC

http://www.amazon.com/dp/B00BKLGB4W

Contents

Disclaimer..2

Unveiling Samsung Galaxy S4 3

Introducing Samsung Galaxy S4 7

   The Mesmerizing Layout..9

   Galaxy S4 Key Specifications 11

Getting to Know Samsung S4 Inside and Out 13

   Learning the Basic Features...14

      Smart Screen..14

      Air View...19

      S Voice...24

      Samsung Account...28

   Discovering Screen Lock Options 33

      Face Unlock..33

      Face and Voice Unlock..37

      Swipe, Pattern and Pin:..40

      Further Screen Lock Options...40

   Galaxy S4 Communication Skills 44

      ChatOn..44

   Connectivity 53

      S Beam...53

   S4 Exclusive Services..58

      S Health...58

      S Translator...65

      Samsung Hub 68

      Samsung WatchOn..72

   Multimedia and Entertainment Options of Galaxy S4..80

      Pop Up Video Multitasking 80

      Music Player...82

      Group Play..84

      Story Album..85

      S Memo 86

      Camera 87

Settings..88

    Air Gestures..88

    Motion Settings..91

    My Places Setup 93

    Power Saving Mode 98

Bottom Line: Grab Yours Now! 100

Introducing Samsung Galaxy

S4

Samsung has launched its fourth member of its 'Galaxy S series'. This time the South Korean manufacturer has introduced its first camera-focused Android smartphone. Introducing a 16 megapixel camera with 16x optical zoom, CMOS Sensor, Xenon Flash and Optical Image Stabiliser, this could be the perfect device for the real photography enthusiasts.

Samsung Galaxy S4 provides high quality mobile entertainment and effective communication using Samsung's technological expertise and high standards. This guide is especially designed to detail the smart device's exclusive features and functions to help you get started with your magic machine.

The Mesmerizing Layout

Check out the beautifully designed Galaxy S4 and its exterior features.

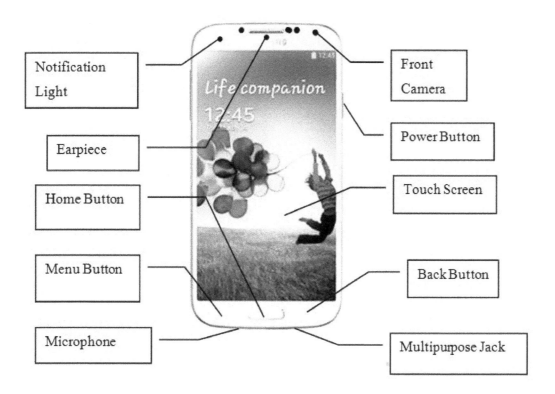

Notification Light

Front Camera

Earpiece

Power Button

Home Button

Touch Screen

Menu Button

Back Button

Microphone

Multipurpose Jack

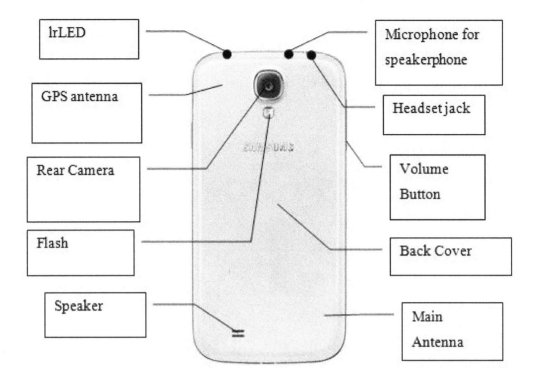

IrLED

GPS antenna

Rear Camera

Flash

Speaker

Microphone for speakerphone

Headset jack

Volume Button

Back Cover

Main Antenna

Note: The microphone for speakerphone is only active when you take videos or activate speakerphone during a call.

Galaxy S4 Key Specifications

Want to know the exclusive specifications of your Galaxy s4 in a glance? Check out the list of key specifications below:

Highlights

- Super AMOLED complete HD, 5 inch 1080p Display
- Exynos 5 Octa Core Processor
- Bluetooth 4.0
- Floating Touch
- 13MP Camera

Battery

- Capacity – 2500 mAh
- Talktime – 1020 mins
- Standby – 370 hours

Camera/Video

- Camera -13MP
- Zoom – yes
- Resolution – 4208 x 3120
- Flash – yes
- Secondary camera – yes
- Video out – yes

Media

- Audio playback – yes

- Ringtones – 64 polyphonic, MP3, WAV, MIDI, AMR

- Video playback – yes

- FM Radio – No

- Headphone jack 3.5mm – yes

Memory

- Inbuilt – 16 GB

- Memory Slot – Yes microSD/TransFlash

Getting to Know Samsung S4

Inside and Out

Discover everything you need to know about Galaxy S4 and get started with this outstanding

phone with the step by step guide, tips and tricks covered in this book. Learn how to operate your

phone effectively, use hand gestures for Air Browsing, utilize multiple window option at one

time, and operate Samsung Hub and a lot more.

Learning the Basic Features

Learn what Samsung Galaxy S4 is all about and start from the basics.

Smart Screen

Samsung Galaxy S4 exclusively features **Smart Screen** function. This feature simplifies your display management settings, where you can select interactions mode with your smart device. Access the settings for **Smart Screen** by tapping Menu button followed by **Settings**.

Select **My Device** in the **Settings Menu** on top and Select **Smart Screen** option

There are further four features behind Smart Screen – **Smart Stay**, **Smart Rotation**, **Smart Pause** and **Smart Scroll**.

The **Smart Stay** feature utilized the front camera to detect your face and eyes to analyse when you are using your device. Regardless of your screen timeout setting, your phone will not turn off while you are looking at it. To activate this feature, tap **Smart Stay** and touch **OK**.

The **Smart Rotation** also sense when you are looking at the device with the front camera to keep the screen from rotating depending on the orientation of your face. To active, tap **Smart Rotation** and select **OK.**

The **Smart Pause** feature is really interesting and will pause your device at the point when you will look away from your device. Again, your device senses your movement through the front camera. Activate **Smart Pause** by tapping over the option and clicking **OK.**

On the basis of your device's angle, The **Smart Scroll,** with the help of its front camera, scrolls through page such as web pages, lists or messages. For activating this amazing feature, tap the slider that displays **Off** to turn it **On.** Tap on the Smart Scroll again to view further **Smart Scroll** options.

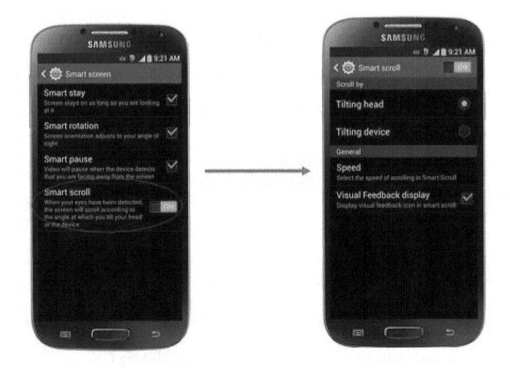

As can be seen in the illustration above, there are further four options that you need to adjust here – **Tilting Head, Tilting Device, Speed** and **Visual Feedback Display.**

Tilting Head is the default setting. The smart scroll is based on the orientation of your face with respect to the device with the help of the front camera.

Exactly the opposite, **Tilting Device** activation scroll is based on your device's orientation in relation with your face movement with the help of the front camera.

Speed refers to the scrolling speed which can be adjusted accordingly. Tap the **Speed** option and adjust the slider towards the right or left to increase or decrease the speed of scrolling, respectively.

By marking the checkbox of **Visual Feedback Display** you will see a visual feedback icon as you use the **Smart Control** feature.

With this last step, you have successfully learnt using the **Smart Screen** feature.

Air View

Air View is an exclusive Galaxy S4 feature that enables the user to interact with their personal smart device without touching it. The feature enables you preview mails, messages, and other files and details, movie or video timeline, contacts assigned on speed dial, as well as magnifying effects on webpages.

To use **Air View** effectively, hover or hold your finders at a slight distance from the screen for a few moments without the need of physically touching the screen. To turn on the **Air View** tap menu button and go to **Settings.**

Tap on **My Device,** scroll down and tap the **Air View** option to proceed.

The **Air View** slider is off by default. Touch the slider on the top to **Turn On** the feature. Once all the sliders appear on the screen, touch each feature of the slider to **Turn On.**

Since **Air View** has several features, you can tap on any feature name to check out the detailed

tutorial. For instance, check out the first feature **Information Preview.** Tap on the feature and

tap **Try** to view the tutorial.

Hover over a specific date associated with events to open up the expanded display window. Tap on the **Back Key** to return to the previous menu.

Repeat the process for all the features available under **Air View.**

Next, tap the **Sound and Haptic Feedback** option under the **Additional Feedback** feature to enable vibration and sound effects when using the **Air View** items through hovering.

The **Air View** feature has been successfully completed!

S Voice

The amazing Samsung S Voice app enables you to perform operations on your phone with your voice. Instead of using your hands to dial numbers, play music or sending a message, you can command your device with your voice to do so. Want to use Samsung S Voice Application? Go through the steps below:

Touch **Apps** on the **Home Screen** and follow to the next page and tap **S Voice.**

Next, you will see a Disclaimer page and Terms of Service Page, which you must accept in order to proceed to the actual application. Once you are through, you will see the **About S Voice** screen. By tapping on **Next,** you will be guided through the tutorial for the app.

Note: You can touch **Skip** right next to the **Next** button to skip tutorial and begin using the application.

The next page is **Say What You Want** and that's exactly what you are going to do with this feature. Tap **Next** and review the available information on the next page, **Wake Up S Voice,** and press **Next** again to continue.

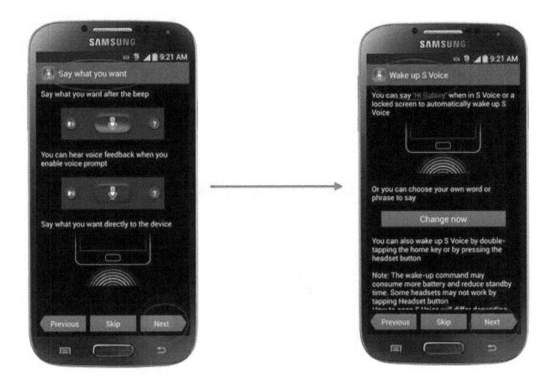

The next screen is **Edit What You Said**. Here, you need to review the information and tap **Next** to proceed to the **Help** menu. There is a list of options available here. All these can be checked one by one to learn how to use **S Voice** feature. Once all the features are reviewed, click **Finish.**

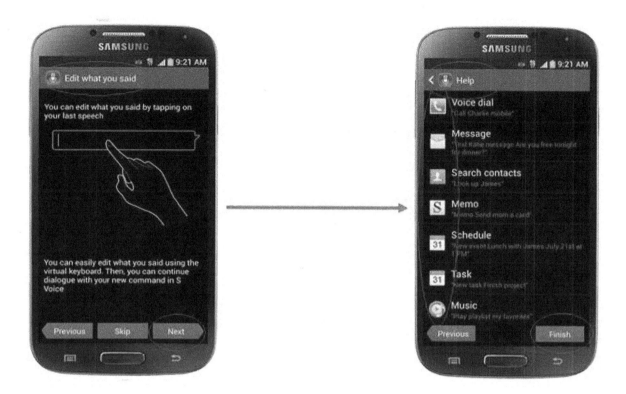

Try each option on this page one by one and speak to your phone to give commands. Try all options and find out how effectively your phone listens to you. Once you are done checking all of them, use this feature to command your phone with voice, effortlessly.

Samsung Account

In order to access all the exclusive features of your Samsung's smartphone, you need to have **Samsung Account.** With an account, you can easily keep your personal information in backup as well as restore supported device.

The option of creating a Samsung account is prompted during the initial setup of Samsung Galaxy S4. If you didn't create your account then, create one now using the following steps:

Go to **Menu** followed by the **Settings** option. Next, go to **Accounts option** and tap **Add Account** from the given options on the page.

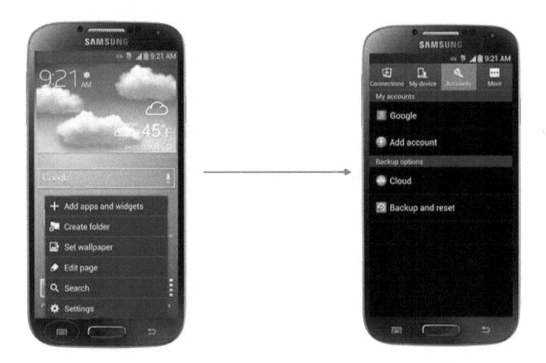

You will see another list of options. Tap **Samsung Account** from the list to continue.

The next screen will give you the option to **Sign In** using your existing account as well as a

Create New Account option. You can continue using the **Sign In** option if you have already

setup **Samsung Account.**

To create a new Samsung account, tap on **Create New Account** and proceed to the next screen where you will be asked to enter your personal details, username and password. Also check the **Receive Newsletter** to stay updated on new services, features and content.

Tap **Sign Up** to proceed.

The next screen displays the terms and conditions for **Samsung Account.** Review all the policies, conditions and terms and check '**I Accept All the Terms above'** checkbox to continue.

Tap on **Check for Verification email** on the next screen to access your email. Until the verification step is not followed, your **Samsung Account** will not be activated.

Touch **Confirm** to complete the account setup process and return to the **Accounts Screen**. You

have successfully learnt to setup your **Samsung Account.**

Discovering Screen Lock Options

Your Samsung Galaxy S4 is your private magic machine that will remain guarded with the plenty of **Screen Lock** options. Check out your S4 exclusive options in this chapter and chose which one would you like to keep for your device.

Face Unlock

Face Unlock is a screen lock option that you can use to protect your phone from unauthorised access. To use **Face Unlock** feature, tap the **Menu** option on your Home Screen and go to **Setting** followed by **My Device** and touch **Lock Screen** option from the list.

There are further options on the next screen. Tap on **Screen Lock** to continue. Choose the **Face Unlock** option and proceed.

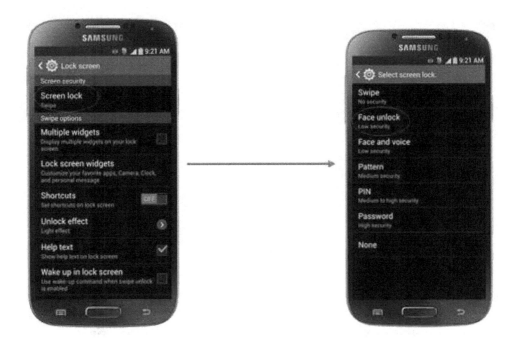

Proceed to the next **Warning Screen** and review the information. Tap on **Next** to review the

Face Unlock message prompt and tap **Set it Up.**

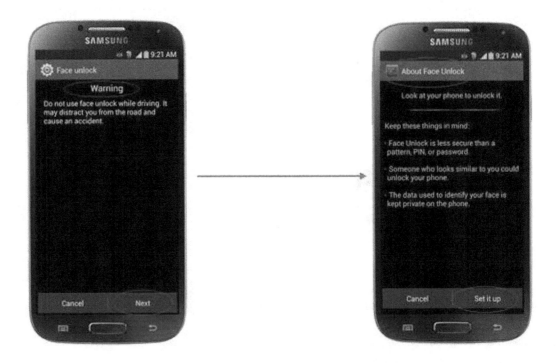

The next screen will guide you through some tips **For Best Results.** After reading, tap **Continue** to proceed.

Adjust your front camera to your face properly so that it appears inside the dotted line. This is where the device will be able to recognize your face. Once the Face Captured screen appears, tap **Continue** to proceed to the next screen.

Next, you'll be asked to create a backup **Pattern** or **Pin.** For example, you choose to go with backing up this lock feature with a **Pin.** Touch **Pin** and enter a pin number. Touch **Continue** and you will be required to enter the same pin code again.

Click Ok and **You're All Done!**

Face and Voice Unlock

Face and Voice Unlock feature is similar to the **Face Unlock** feature with addition of voice

recognition function. Tap **Menu,** go to **Settings** followed by **My Device** and tap **Lock Screen**

option (same steps mentioned above). In the **Screen Lock** option list, tap **Face and Voice** option

to continue.

Similar to **Face Unlock** option, you will next see a warning page that you must read thoroughly

before proceeding to avoid issues later. Tap **Set It Up** to continue. Review the points for best

results and tap **Continue** to jump to the next screen. Follow the same steps to adjust your face

within the dotted line to enable your device to recognize your face to unlock. Tap **Continue** to

setup voice settings.

Voice setup could be tricky, but if you follow the steps correctly, you will have a much stronger

password for your device. Tap the **Microphone Icon** on the **Voice Setup Screen.**

You need to record your voice command 4 times in a row to set it as your voice password. Once it's recorded, you will be automatically redirected to the next screen. Click **Done** to continue or **Reinforce** to record all over again.

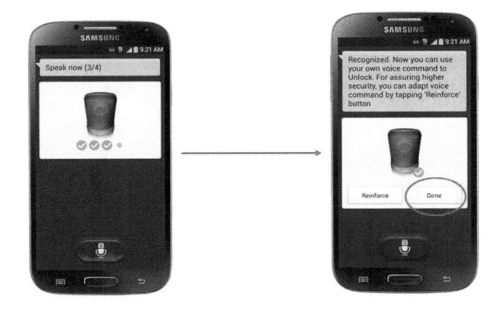

As you did in the **Face Unlock** feature, set a backup pin or password for your **Face and Voice Unlock** feature as well. Follow the same steps and your phone will not allow access unless and until it sees you and hears you, both.

Swipe, Pattern and Pin:

Further Screen Lock Options

Swipe, Pattern and Pin are the common ways of locking up your screen. Learn how you'll do it on your Samsung Galaxy S4.

Swipe Option

Get back to your **Screen Lock** option, following the same method. Tap **Swipe** option from the list to continue with this option. This is indeed a great lock feature to keep your phone from opening applications because of its sensitive touch screen or making accidental calls. However, for security purpose, this feature may not be helpful at all.

Clicking **Swipe** will automatically turn it on. To unlock, touch **Swipe** from the **Screen Lock Menu.**

Pattern Option

Go to **Settings** from the **Menu** followed by **My Devices** option on the top and select **Patterns** from the **Screen Lock** list. On the next screen, you will find 9 dots that you can utilize to make a pattern. You can utilize all the dots or just a few of them to set a pattern. Once you have drawn the pattern of your choice, tap **Continue** to proceed to the next screen. The example can be seen in the picture below.

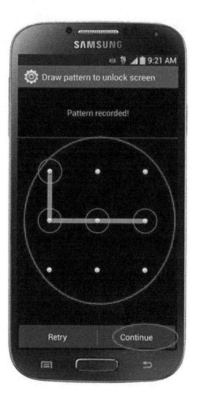

You will be prompted to draw the same pattern on the next screen for confirmation. Draw the same pattern and click on the **Confirm** button present at the bottom of the screen. Remember, you can always hit **Retry** button to choose another pattern.

Next, you will be prompted to set a backup pin code. This pin code will help you unlock your phone in case you forget the pattern. Tap **Continue** to move to the next page.

Re-enter the pin code on the next screen tap **OK** to successfully finish setting up your **Pattern Lock.**

Pin Option

From the **Screen Lock** menu, select the **Pin** option. Enter the numeric pin and tap **Continue** to proceed to the next screen.

You will be prompted to enter the pin again to confirm. Enter the same pin and tap **OK.** Your pin

has successfully been set as your screen lock.

Galaxy S4 Communication Skills

Galaxy S4 has great 'Communication Skills', which will keep you connected with the online world through this smart device. Read on and learn more about it.

ChatOn

Communicate with your friends and family regardless of their device types or platforms. ChatOn is available for all major web browsers and mobile platforms. Using ChatOn, you can share videos and photos with the help of the Trunk feature, while chatting with your friends and family.

Tap the **Apps** option to open your Galaxy S4 applications.

To use **ChatOn,** you need to access it using your **Samsung Account** (setup mentioned earlier)**.**
If you are not already signed in, tap **Sign In**, enter your account details. When on the main
screen after signing in, touch **Next** to continue.

On the next screen, a text field will be provided to you to enter your name. This name will be
displayed on your **ChatOn** application for your friends to recognize you. Enter your name and
tap on the **Check** on the top right of the screen to proceed.

With this step, you will enter the main screen of the **ChatOn** application. Next, add a friend to your list by tapping the **Menu** button and selecting **Add Buddy** option. Tap on **Contact Sync** button to continue.

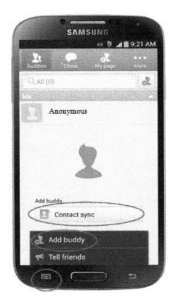

You will be prompted to enter your **Country Code** and **Phone Number** on the next screen. Add

the details and tap Voice if you wish to receive a voice call for verification code or tap **SMS** to

receive a text message with a 4-digit code for verification.

Once you receive the verification code, enter it onto the next screen and tap **Next.** You can also

request for a verification code in case you didn't receive in the next three minutes.

Next, you will be prompted that all the contacts in your **Samsung Account** will be imported on to the application and will be added as friends on Facebook. If you like, you can also check the checkbox for **Include SIM Contacts** to allow **ChatOn** to incorporate your sim contacts too. Tap **OK** to continue.

In the tabs mentioned above, tap **Tell Friends** tab to send a link to your friends so that they can install ChatOn on their smart devices.

Touch the next tab that says **Phone Number** to search for your friends through their contact

numbers. This can turn out to be really effective sometimes.

The next tab is the **Search by ID** tab. Move to this tab and search for your friends by entering Samsung email address of your friend to search for them on the database of **ChatOn.** Tap the **Search** icon to start looking.

Once the search results appear, tap the **Plus** icon on the corner of the screen to add the contact.

To begin chatting, tap the **Chats** tab on the top of the screen, right next to the **Buddies** tap, where you can see all your friends and their availability statuses. On the next screen you will see a **Start Chat** option. Tap on the option to check which friends are available.

To select the friend you would like to chat with, check the checkbox in front of that friend's name. Tap the **Right Mark** on top right of the screen to start chatting.

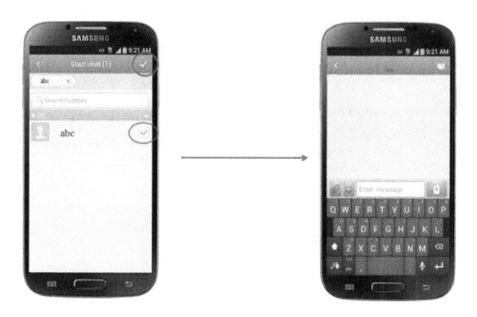

Tap back button on top of the chat screen to come back to the **Chat Menu.** If you wish to send a message to your entire contact list, tap **Broadcast** and continue.

You have successfully learnt to use the **ChatOn** feature.

Connectivity

The S Beam application is fast and easy to use. This efficient **Connectivity** application lets you share content with other smart devices using Wi-Fi Direct or NFC.

Still don't know how to use the amazing S Beam feature in your Galaxy S4? Check out the step by step guide below.

S Beam

Before **S Beam** feature can be used, it needs to be turned on. To do so, tap **Menu** at home page and go to **Settings.**

Under the **Connectivity** tab right on the next screen, you will see **S Beam** in the list under the

Connect and Share heading. Tap on the feature to proceed.

The feature is turnedd off by default. You need to tap the **Slider** to turn the feature **On.** When **S**

Beam is turned on, Tap the **Home** button to go back to the home screen. It is important to

remember that for successful sharing of content, it is important that the feature is turned on in

both the devices.

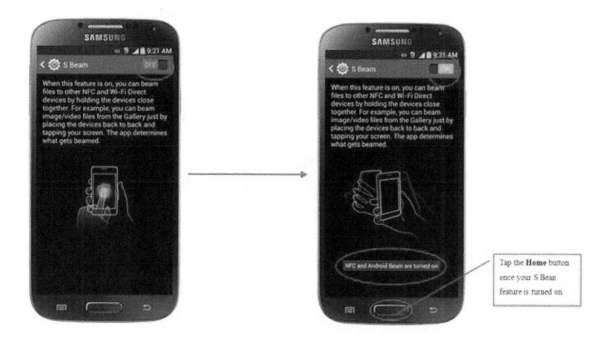

Now that the feature is turned on, it is time to use it. To begin, touch **Apps** on the Home Screen and visit your **Gallery** by tapping on it. (In this example, we will share pictures with another device using **S Beam**).

Tap on a specific **Folder** with a picture you wish to share. Tap the **Picture.**

Next, you need to do some action. Touch the two devices together, again and again. Once the sending device shows **Touch to Beam,** tap on the screen and start the beaming procedure.

Next, your device will prompt you to separate the device so that it starts sending the content. Separating the device will instantly begin transfering the file or content.

You can see the trasfered content on the receiving device's screen after the transfer is complete.

This process is easy to follow and the transfer rate is faster than other transferring options.

S4 Exclusive Services

Want to know what Galaxy S4 brings for you? This chapter covers the exclusive S4 services in detail. Keep reading.

S Health

Wish you had a personal health management powerhouse? Your wish will come true as soon as you have Samsung Galaxy S4 in your hand. With this exclusive application, you can track various health statistics, like blood glucose levels, blood pressure, and weight. The environmental conditions can be tracked, and you can even input your exercise routine.

To use this feature, open the app by tapping **Apps** from the **Home Screen** and select **S Health.**

On the welcome screen, tap **Next** and proceed with the application.

Next, you will come across the **Terms of Use** page. Check the **Agree** box in the **Use of Health**

section. Also, mark the checkbox for **Connection Third Party Devices** and **Programs** sections.

Last but not the least you must also check the checkbox under the **Information Used** section.

Touch **Next** to continue to the next screen.

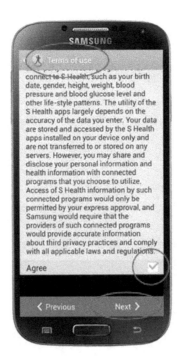

The next screen will prompt you to enter your profile details. This includes your Name, Weight, Height, Birthday, Sex and Activity Type. Touch Start to continue to the next screen.

The next screen is the **Health Board.** It displays the statistics of the current day and gives results in a graphical format. The next time you will open S Health, the **Health Board** will be your main screen. Tap the **Graph** icon on the bottom of the screen to view an example.

After looking at the graph, hit the back key and tap on the **Health Board Options** on top of the

screen to explore more features of **S Health. S Health** features **Walking Mate,** a built-in

counter. Turn this feature on, carry your device with you in your pocket and start walking. The

number of steps you walk will be recorded by the device.

Touch **Walking Mate** from the menu and tap **Start to begin.**

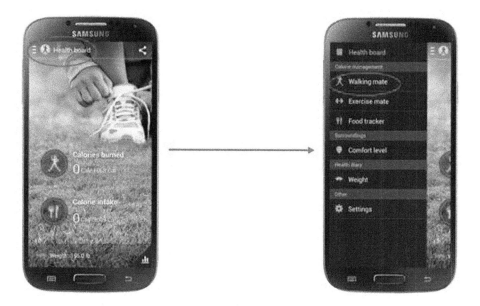

The next feature on the list is **Exercise Mate.** It helps you track your exercise regime and activities. There are a number of preloaded exercises that will help you track your calories burned. Tap **Enter** to start a new activity.

Next, try out the **Food Tracker** feature. It provides you the most efficient and easy way to track and record your daily food consumption and lets you know how many calories are remaining for you to consume of your planned daily consumption.

Tap **Food Tracker** from the menu to access this smart feature.

Check out all the remaining functions of **S Health** to learn the most effective and efficient use of this amazing application.

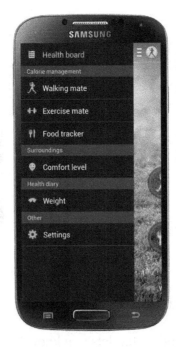

S Translator

Samsung's very own **S Translator** is a quick and easy way to translate entered text or spoken words into various different languages. Samsung Galaxy S4 supports English (USA and UK), Chinese, German, French, Japanese, Korean, Italian, Spanish and Portuguese (Latin America).

S Translator can be accessed from the **Home Screen.** Tap **Apps** and continue.

You have different language options available in the drop menu. You must select a language in the top and bottom boxes. You can translate text or audio between the two languages entered here. Enter text in any box to translate into another language.

You can also give audio commands to the application to translate into another language. Tap the

Voice button on the right side of the screen to continue. You may be prompted to download high

quality voice file. Tap **OK** to proceed.

Follow the instructions to download the voice files.

It is also possible to save translations as favorites. So, when you are done with a translation, tap the **Start Icon** on the top right of the screen to add it to your favorites.

Now you know how to use this amazing Samsung Galaxy S4 feature.

Samsung Hub

Your phone will suddenly become your central marketplace, which provides you access to a number of mobile content, such as music, games, videos and books. Again, you need to have a **Samsung Account** to use this feature. To access **Samsung Hub**, this is what you need to do:

Tap **Apps** on the **Home Screen** and select **Samsung Hub** from the list of applications.

You can access the featured content on the 'What's New' screen. Slide you finger over the screen to check out what **Samsung Hub** has to offer.

Tap the **Samsung Help** icon on the right corner of the screen to return to the main page.

You can sweep and slide and get into the categories in detail to gain a clear idea about what you

can get from this place. As soon as you come across anything you wish to buy, navigate and tap

Get to download the game , music, video or book to your device.

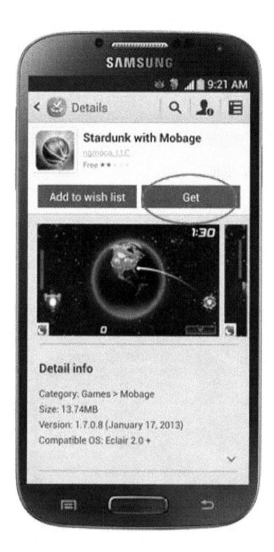

With the plethora of options available here, you will definitely witness that it's a complete HUB

of entertainment offered by Samsung Galaxy S4!

Samsung WatchOn

If you love watching TV, this application will definitely entertain you. Get the TV viewing experience with **Samsung WatchOn.** You can discover, search, explore and access TV shows and movies on demand. The on-demand video can be watched on your smart device, while you can also choose to watch it on a compatible television set.

Learn how to make the most out of it with the steps below:

First of all, access the app by tapping **Apps** on the Home Screen and then touch **WatchOn** icon.

Using **WatchOn** for the first time will take you through a Setup Wizard. First, you will be

prompted to **Select Your Country/Region.** This will help you in configuring your television or

other devices.

You will see a list of countries on the screen. Choose yours to continue. Also, enter your zip

code and tap **Done.**

You will be directed to the next page where you will see a list of TV service providers according to your Zip Code. Choose yours and proceed.

The next option you'll come across is interesting. This feature gives you a chance to personalize what you what. Select personalize on the next screen and continue. There is a list genre that you can reorder according to your preference. Drag and relocate to adjust.

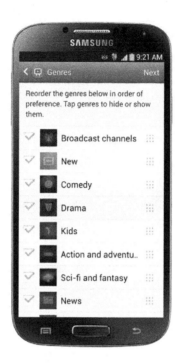

Enter your Gender and Age on the next screen and tap **We Value Your Privacy** and choose your preferred browser to view the Privacy Policy of **WatchOn.** Click **Done.**

Agree to the **Samsung Disclaimer** to proceed. Also tap on **Agree** button after reviewing the Peel disclaimer.

Next, setup your device by touching the **Remote** icon on the top right of the screen so that your phone controls your set-top box, TV, DVR, DVD players, Blue-ray and other electronic devices. On the next screen, Tap **Set up Now** when prompted.

You will see the list of TV brand on your device. If you do not see your TV brand on the list, tap **Other TV Brand.** Tap **I Have a Projector** to check the list of available projector brands. In this example, tap your TV brand and continue.

For example, if you have a Samsung TV and your device has recognized it, tap the **Power** button on the bottom of the screen to turn on your television. In case your TV does not display an image, tap **Retry** on the next prompt screen. If your TV turns on, tap **Yes** to proceed. Remember, some televisions can take up to several seconds before displaying an image.

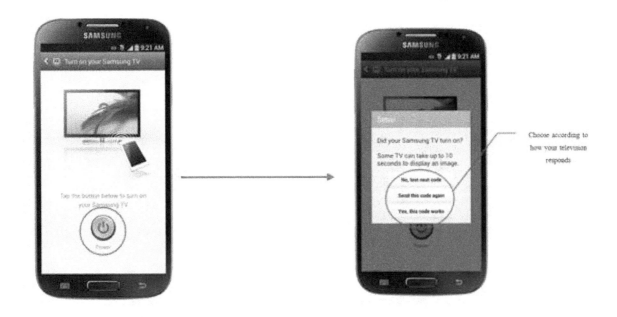

On the next screen, input the method you use to change channels. If you choose

Satellite/Cable/PVR/STB/DVR, a complete guide will be provided to help you in choosing your

brand and setting up your smartphone to control the satellite box/cable. For this example, we will

tap **My Samsung TV. WatchOn** is ready to be used!

Multimedia and Entertainment Options of Galaxy S4

This spectacular smart machine is your complete entertainment package. The Multimedia and Entertainment Options of Galaxy S4 are indeed endless. Check the exclusive ones below:

Pop Up Video Multitasking

Your smart device features **Pop Up Video Multitasking,** which enables you to multitask while watching a video on your phone. To learn how to go about with it, first of all play a video from the **Samsung Video** or **Gallery.** When the video is playing, you will see a small **Pop Up Icon** on the right bottom corner of the screen. By touching that tap, your video will suddenly get into a smaller window and will remain on your screen.

The small window can be touched and dragged to any area of the screen. Press the **Home** button to open any other app from the list. You can also touch the video window to pause it while you perform another activity on your phone. The video playing in the smaller video on your **Home** screen can also be directly closed using the small 'x' on the window.

Music Player

The **Music Player** enables the S4 users to play music with the files and tracks stored on the micro SD card or device. Music player application is available on the application list on your device. This app has two basic views: the **Now Playing** view and the **Library View.** Your **Music Player** is set on the library view by default.

The list of songs is right on your screen when you are in the default view. Just tap the song you wish to listen to. The song will instantly start playing with all the basic controls accessible at the bottom of the screen.

You can view the **Album Art** on the bottom left corner of the screen. By touching the screen here, you will shift to the **Now Playing** view. Here you have four different tabs on the top of the screen: Songs, Playlist, Albums and Artists.

The **Songs** tab will show you the list of all the tracks you have in your device. By tapping on **Playlist**, you will be taken to the playlist setup. The **Album** and **Artist** tabs, you can choose a particular song without a lot of navigation.

Enjoy your **Music Player!**

Group Play

Group Play is an amazing feature that enables multiple people to share and access content on one platform. Just select the content you wish to share using the touchscreen feature on your phone. The markup is displayed to everyone as soon as you share anything. **Group Play** enables you to share photos, documents, music and even lets you play games using the app.

Go to **Group Play** in the applications list. Check the **Disclaimer** and tap **OK** to proceed. On the next screen, tap **Create Group** to begin with a new session. You will see your options on the screen. You can choose to share music, pictures, and documents or play games as you like. Tap on your options and select the number of files you want to share.

Enjoy **Group Play!**

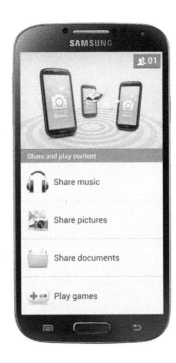

Story Album

Do you wish to organize your photos more appropriately and give it a shape of an album? You can do this on your Galaxy S4 smartphone. Create albums based on events and arrange pictures accordingly. To setup this amazing feature, go to **Apps** list from the **Home Screen** and tap **Story Album.**

Tap **Start** to proceed. The next screen will display a **Create Album Screen** option. Pictures can be selected **From Gallery** or **By Tag information.** The latter option enables you to create an album from specific tag photos. Let's keep to **From Gallery** option for this example.

Go to gallery and select all the pictures you wish to add. Once all the pictures are selected, tap **Done.** Give your photo story album a **Title, Theme** and a **Cover Image** and tap **Create Album.** Enjoy your **Story Album** on your device or get it printed in a hardcopy and secure your memories forever.

S Memo

Stick important memos to your phone. The S Memo application enables you to make memos using your finger as a pen or using the keyboard. This is one application that allows users to use pictures, text and voice recording in one place.

Launch **S Memo** by touching the icon in the **Apps.** You will see a small pen side on top of the screen. Tap this icon to compose a new S Memo. Touch the screen and use your finger as a pen to write the message. There are various toolbars and other options that will help you with S Memo editing.

Select the **T** button next to the **Pen** icon to add text on the **S Memos** using a Keyboard.

Catch up with your priorities and things to do with **S Memo** in your Galaxy S4.

Camera

The directly accessible **Camera** is available on the **Home Screen.** Simply tap on the icon to access the incredible **Camera** of your Galaxy S4. Aim towards the subject and touch the screen on a specific area to identify the focal point. When it turns green touch the **Camera Shutter** button. Your camera offers a wide range of auto mode options that you can check by tapping the thumbnail.

If you wish to access the **Camera's Quick Settings,** check out the viewfinder screen. The settings available for you here will depend on the type of mode you are currently using. The **Video Recording** option is also available here. You may just tap the icon to go to the **Video Recording** mode. You can also try features like **Double Camera** to swap between the back and front cameras. Explore your options and click you memories on all special and casual occasion using your 13 mp camera.

Settings

Now here comes the settings you can't even think of moving ahead without checking out. These exclusive S4 features will indeed amuse you. Check them all out.

Air Gestures

Air Gesture is exclusive to Galaxy S4 and is a great feature that helps you control your smartphone with specific hand movements above the screen and commands the phone without touching it.

To use **Air Gesture** feature, touch **Menu** on the **Home Screen** and tap **Settings.** Select **Motions and Gestures** under the **My Devices** tab.

Motion and Gestures offer three different types. For this example, we will check out the **Air Gesture** feature. There is a slider right next to the **Air Gesture** feature, which you need to tap in order to turn it **On**.

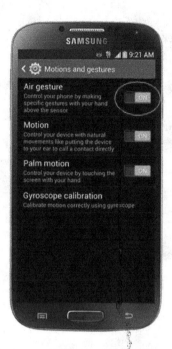

Next, touch the **Air Gesture** name and tap on **Air Jump** option to go through a quick tutorial on using this feature.

After going through the tutorial, you can even try using the feature on your own by tapping **Try**

It.

At the end of the trial, you will have a fair idea about what **Air Gesture** is all about.

Motion Settings

Motion settings also fall under the **Motion and Gesture** Setting. This enables you to control your phone with natural device movements, or touching/moving the screen. The initial steps would remain the same and you must navigate all the way to the **Motion and Gestures** main screen. However, this time, tap **Motion** instead of air gesture to turn it **On.**

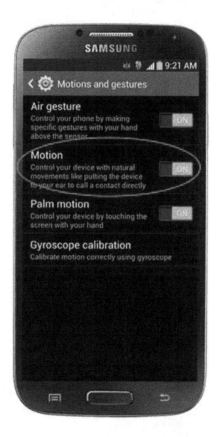

Touch the name **Motion** again to explore the options. Learn how to use the motion gestures effectively by going through a useful, quick tutorial. For this example, let's check out **Direct Call** option.

Use the feature yourself after you are done with the detailed tour by tapping **Try It** on the next

prompt.

My Places Setup

Setting up **My Places** is important because this feature enables you device to identify your location and give you relevant services and information. Add places using Bluetooth, Wi-Fi or Maps to recognize location.

For **My Places Setup** go to **Menu** followed by **Settings** and tap on the **More** tab at the end. Select **Location Services** from the list to continue.

Tap **My Places** from the list.

The next screen will give you a chance to add places. You can tap the **Plus** sign on the top right to add a new place or can choose from the three predefined options available on the screen. To continue with this example, we will tap **Office.**

Next, tap the **Select Method,** to choose the feature you wish to utilize to define the particular

location.

Select **Map** to make use of the **GPS Information** to define a specific location. Select **Wi-Fi** or

Bluetooth for defining the location by its Wi-Fi access point connection or through Bluetooth.

Tap **Map** in this example.

Each method has its own set of rules. You must provide proper Bluetooth and/or Wi-Fi. When

choosing Map, you may need to look out for your own location with the help of current GPS

coordinates. Enter your location and tap **Search** icon and tap the **Tick** to proceed.

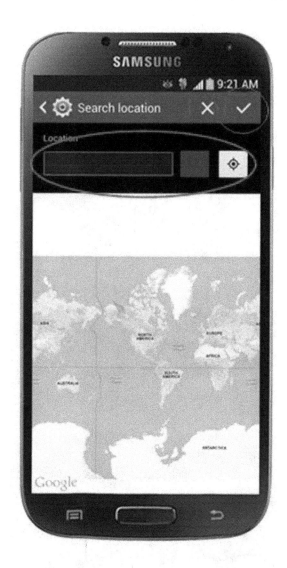

Tap the **Tick** again to save new **My Places.**

Power Saving Mode

Conserve your smartphone's battery by taking it to the **Power Saving Mode.** Touch **Menu** and go to **Settings**. Tap **My Devices** tab and select **Power Saving Mode.**

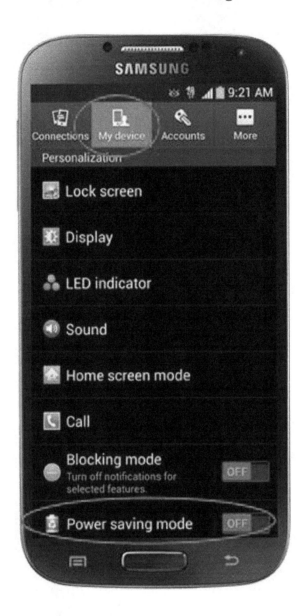

On the next screen, touch the slider in front of the **Power Saving Mode** option, to turn it **On.**

The power saving settings can be adjusted according to you own requirement. There are options that you can check or uncheck for the settings. The tip here is to **Turn Off Haptic Feedback** option to conserve battery power.

This step has been completed successfully!

Bottom Line: Grab Yours Now!

This book is your complete guide to getting started with your Samsung Galaxy S4. This mesmerizing phone has been launched and is available in the market for you. Put your hands over the latest Samsung Galaxy S generation and make the most out of the exclusive features especially designed for your generation.

Now that you are familiar with the exclusive features of this amazing machine, using your phone to its fullest will not be a problem for you. If you have already bought one, start exploring its spectacular features, and if you are still deciding to get one, it's high time you grab yours now!

Enjoy every bit of your Samsung Galaxy S4 ownership!

Other Titles By This Author Include...

http://www.amazon.com/dp/B00ALC9OHC

http://www.amazon.com/dp/B00BKLGB4W